197898

Talking Hands

QUESTIONS AND ANSWERS

PREGUNTAS Y RESPUESTAS

WRITTEN BY KATHLEEN PETELINSEK AND E. RUSSELL PRIMM
ILLUSTRATED BY NICHOLE DAY DIGGINS

A SPECIAL THANKS TO OUR ADVISERS: JUNE PRUSAK IS A DEAF THERAPEUTIC RECREATOR WHO
BELIEVES IN THE MOTTO "LIFE IS GOOD," REGARDLESS OF YOUR ABILITY TO HEAR.

CARMINE L. VOZZOLO IS AN EDUCATOR OF CHILDREN WHO ARE DEAF
AND HARD OF HEARING, AS WELL AS THEIR FAMILIES.

The **Child's World**®

Published in the United States of America by The Child's World®
PO Box 326, Chanhassen, MN 55317-0326
800-599-READ
www.childsworld.com

Cover/frontispiece: RubberBall Productions.

Interior: 3, 13, 14, 19—Stockdisc/Getty Images; 4—Brand X Pictures; 5, 6, 11, 12, 15, 16, 20, 22, 23—Photodisc/Getty Images; 7—RubberBall Productions; C Squared Studios/Photodisc/Getty Images; 9, 10—Burke/Triolo Productions/Brand X Pictures; 17—Digital Vision; 18, 21—Comstock Images.

The Child's World®: Mary Berendes, Publishing Director

Editorial Directions, Inc.: E. Russell Primm, Editorial Director; Katie Marsico, Managing Editor; Judith Shiffer, Associate Editor; Caroline Wood, Editorial Assistant; Javier Millán, Proofreader; Cian Laughlin O'Day, Photo Researcher and Selector

The Design Lab: Kathleen Petelinsek, Art Director; Julia Goozen, Art Production

LIBRARY OF CONGRESS CATALOGING-IN-PUBLICATION DATA

Petelinsek, Kathleen.
  Questions and answers = Preguntas y respuestas / by Kathleen Petelinsek and E. Russell Primm.
    p. cm. — (Talking hands)
  In English and Spanish.
  ISBN 1-59296-455-9 (lib. bdg. : alk. paper)
1. American Sign Language—Juvenile literature. 2. Questions and answers—Juvenile literature. I. Title: Preguntas y respuestas. II. Primm, E. Russell, 1958– III. Title.
  HV2476.P477 2006
  419'.7—dc22   2005027109

NOTE TO PARENTS AND EDUCATORS:

The understanding of any language begins with the acquisition of vocabulary, whether the language is spoken or manual. The books in the Talking Hands series provide readers, both young and old, with a first introduction to basic American Sign Language signs. Combining close photo cues and simple, but detailed, line illustration, children and adults alike can begin the process of learning American Sign Language. In addition to the English word and sign for that word, we have included the Spanish word. The addition of the Spanish word is a wonderful way to allow children to see multiple ways (English, Spanish, signed) to say the same word. This is also beneficial for Spanish-speaking families to learn the sign even though they may not know the English word for that object.

Let these books be an introduction to the world of American Sign Language. Most languages have regional dialects and multiple ways of expressing the same thought. This is also true for sign language. We have attempted to use the most common version of the signs for the words in this series. As with any language, the best way to learn is to be taught in person by a frequent user. It is our hope that this series will pique your interest in sign language.

Question
Pregunta

1.

Draw a question mark in the air from signer's perspective.

Dibuje un signo de interrogación en el aire de la perspectiva del firmante.

3

Answer
Respuesta

1.

2.

4

What?
¿Qué?

1.

2.

Another way to say "What?"

Otra manera de decir "¿Qué?"

1.

5

Who?
¿Quién?

1.

Wiggle index finger.
Menee el dedo índice.

When?
¿Cuándo?

1.

Right index finger moves in a circle around left index finger.

El dedo índice derecho se mueve en un círculo alrededor del dedo índice izquierdo.

Yesterday
Ayer

1.

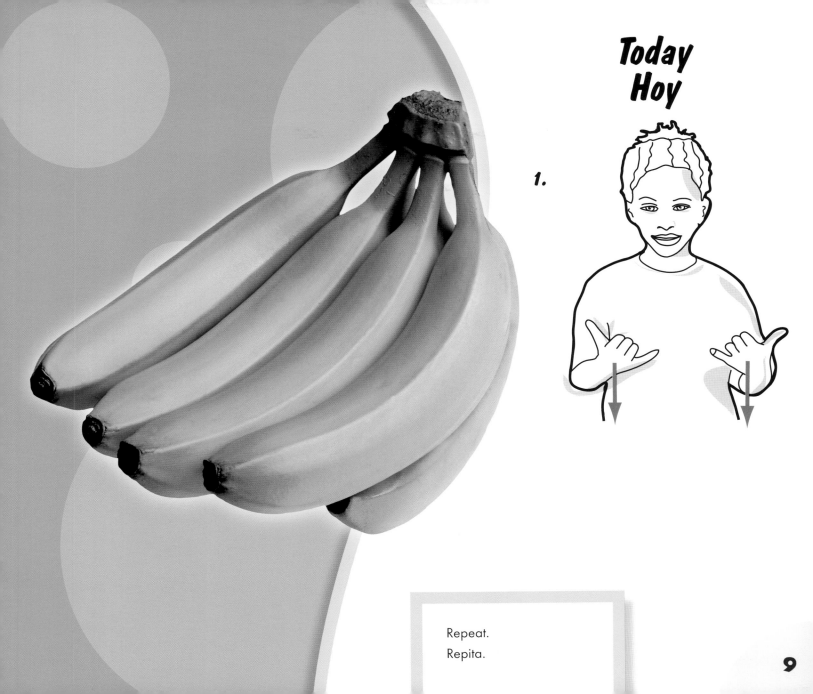

Today
Hoy

1.

Repeat.
Repita.

Tomorrow
Mañana

1.

2.

Where?
¿Dónde?

1.

Here
Aquí

1.

Hands move in circles. Repeat.

Las manos se mueven en círculos. Repita.

12

There
Allí

1.

Point to the object or place.
Apunta hacia el objeto o lugar.

13

Can I?
¿Puedo?

1.

2.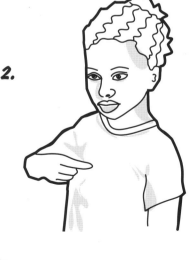

Will you?
¿Puede usted?

1.

2.

3.

For step three, point to person.

Para el paso tres, apunte hacia la persona.

Yes
Sí

1.

Move fist downward at wrist while nodding head yes.

Mueva el puño hacia abajo en la muñeca mientras que cabecea la cabeza sí.

No
No

1.

2.

Touch index and middle fingers of right hand to thumb while shaking head no.

Toque el dedo índice y el dedo medio de la mano derecha mientras que sacude la cabeza no.

17

How?
¿Cómo?

1.

2.

Turn hands upward.

Dé vuelta a las manos hacia arriba.

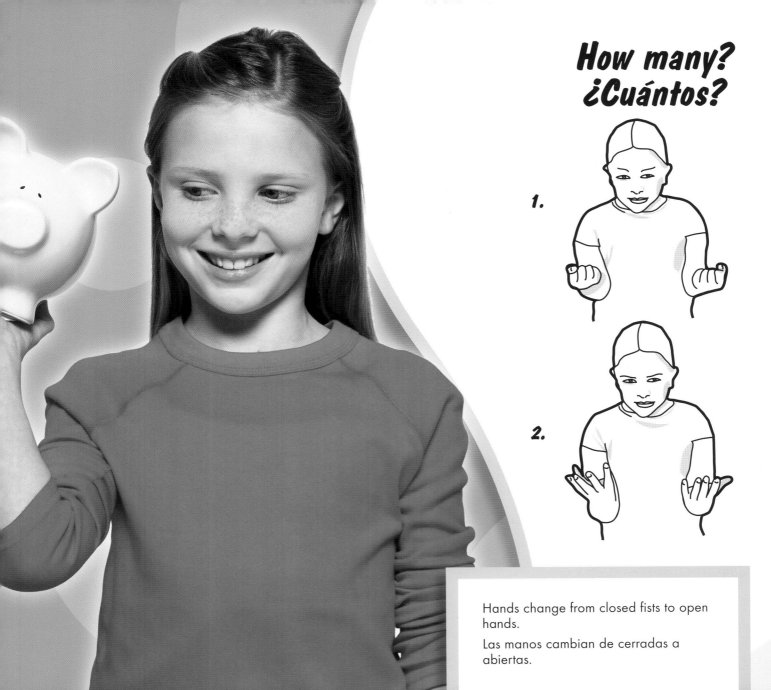

How many?
¿Cuántos?

1.

2.

Hands change from closed fists to open hands.

Las manos cambian de cerradas a abiertas.

19

All
Todos

1.

2.

3.

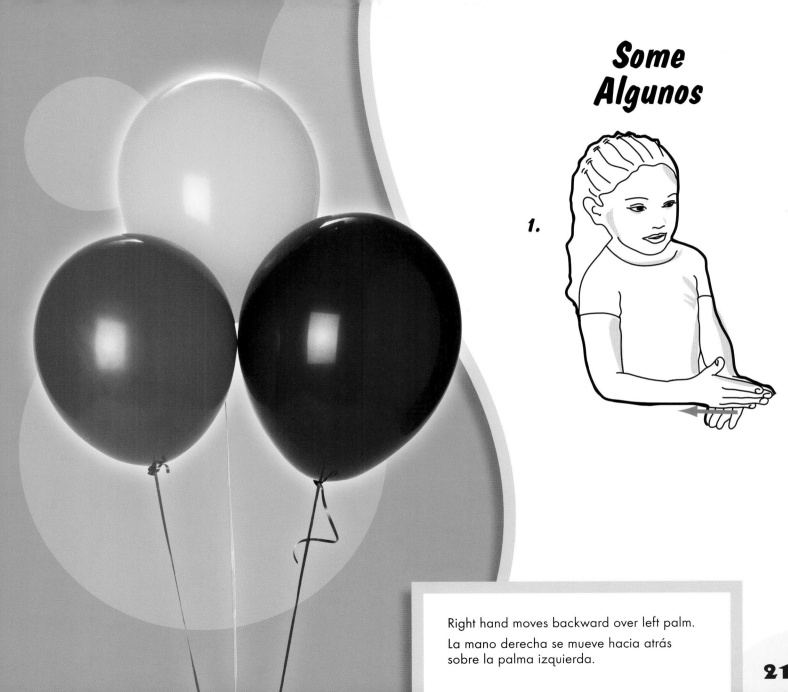

Some
Algunos

1.

Right hand moves backward over left palm.

La mano derecha se mueve hacia atrás
sobre la palma izquierda.

None
Ninguno

1.

Round hands move away from body.

Las manos redondas se mueven lejos del cuerpo.

Why?
¿Por qué?

1.

Wiggle middle finger.
Menee el dedo medio.

A B C D E F

G H I J K

L M N O P

Q R S T U

V W X Y Z

A SPECIAL THANK-YOU

to our models from the Alexander Graham Bell Elementary School in Chicago, Illinois:

Alina is seven years old and is in the second grade. Her favorite things to do are art, soccer, and swimming. DJ is her brother!

Dareous has seven brothers and sisters. He likes football. His favorite team is the Detroit Lions. He also likes to play with his Gameboy and Playstation.

Darionna is seven and is in the second grade. She has two sisters. She likes the swings and merry-go-round on the playground. She also loves art.

DJ is eight years old and is in the third grade. He loves playing the harmonica and his Gameboy. Alina is his sister!

Jasmine is seven years old and is in the second grade. She likes writing and math in school. She also loves to swim.